CLASSIC DREAM CARS

CLASSIC DREAM CARS

MAGNA BOOKS
A Bison Book

Published by Magna Books
Magna Road
Wigston
Leicester, LE8 2ZH

Produced by Bison Books Ltd
176 Old Brompton Road
London SW5 0BA
England

ISBN 0 948509 51 1

Printed and bound in Spain by
Gráficas Estella, S. A. Navarra.

Design: Yves Le Ray

Originally published as *Voitures Extraordinaires*, © 1988 E.P.A.

CONTENTS

Artz

How to be inimitable . . . The famous dress-designer Ugo Putz-Macherin had been invited by Prince Von Pfaffenheim-Weiniger-Metzingen to his *Jägerhof* in the Bavarian mountains for the opening of the hunting season.

Body-stylist Gunther Artz from Hannover specializes in converting Porsche 928's (above) and 944's (below) into high-performance hatchbacks. These are no back yard conversions; they involve serious engineering and bear no trace whatsoever of improvisation. Artz endows his hatchbacks with a completely redesigned roof. To this is added an ultralight rear hatch with a convex window panel. All of Artz's additions are designed to reflect the lines of the original body and blend in superbly with the existing bodywork. If Porsche decides one day to list a 928S or 944 'station wagon' in its catalogue, it is sure to be designed along the same lines as the Artz.

Ugo, ever conscious of his appearance, had devoted as much care to choosing the right car to drive as he had deciding upon the right tie to wear. And the only car that seemed to really suit the occasion was the Porsche 928S.

When he got up to the Prince's eyrie, Ugo drove round behind the *Jägerhof* to where the other guests' cars were already lined up: the 928S belonging to popular writer Herbert Von Marchenzeit, the 928S belonging to fashionable interior-decorator Ernst Grosschlussel, and the 928S driven by the trendy hairdresser Alois Kopfwasche. Alas, sighed Ugo to himself, it's unbelievable how one 928S looks just like another . . .

Two weeks later, the inimitable Ugo was off for the last golf tournament of the season. After giving the question of which car to take much thought (how tiresomely complicated life could be . . .), Ugo had finally decided to take the Ferrari 308 GTSi. When he arrived at the clubhouse, there lined up before him was Von Marchenzeit's GTSi, beside Grosschlussel's GTSi, beside Kopfwasche's GTSi. All of them just the same red as Ugo's of course.

On his way home after golf, Ugo was still grumbling about this disagreeable surprise; but there was more to come . . .

He was speeding along the fast lane of the autobahn when he noticed an ordinary-looking VW Golf in his rear-view mirror. It was fast approaching. 'I must have been starting to doze,' thought Ugo and jammed his foot hard down on the accelerator. Then he decided that he must already be asleep and dreaming: instead of disappearing as fast as it had suddenly appeared, the little Golf had caught right up to the Ferrari and was imperiously demanding right-of-way, flashing its headlamps. That day, Ugo Putz-Macherin finally learned what humility was. Tail between legs, he moved over to the slow lane and the diabolic Golf flashed past as if it had an urgent appointment with the horizon. Despite the tears in his eyes, Ugo managed to make out the name on the back of the Golf: Artz.

At the wheel was Hannover customizer Gunther Artz, who was indulging in his favorite pastime: spreading panic and doubt on the highways in his little Golf, powered by a Porsche 928S engine.

These demonstrations on the road did much more for Artz's reputation than the most sophisticated advertising campaign. Pretty soon, Ugo Putz-Macherin came knocking at his workshop door. Ugo was never to regret it: thanks to Artz, he was to become the proud owner of a 928S and a 308 GTSi that were truly different.

If Gunther Artz has a specialty, then it is the high-performance hatchback. He dreamed of producing a car to match the famous Aston Martin hatchbacks (they weren't yet called that, of course) of the 1960s. After cutting his teeth on the Audi Quattro and then the Porsche 924, Artz turned his attention to the Porsche 928S. Rather than simply stretching the existing roof, he decided to completely redesign the roof panel so that its lines would blend in perfectly with the rest of the body and reveal no trace of the car's mutant origins. The new roof is reinforced by two transverse hoops. The rear door or hatch is made of ultralight synthetic material and has a slightly convex window panel. When you look at the result that Artz achieved, it is difficult to imagine a 928S hatchback looking any other way.

Added to the intended improvements – more accommodating rear seats and a roomier, more practical luggage compartment – the Artz 'station wagon' provides several extra advantages. Gone is the unbearable hothouse effect that the enormous rear window of the coupé generated in summer. Moreover (and the Artz was not the only car to prove this phenomenon), the hatchback with its severe Kamm-type profile provides much

cleaner aerodynamic lines than the factory-built coupé. The rather abrupt cutoff at the rear enhances straight-line stability far more efficiently than the discreet rear spoiler on the 928S coupé. According to Gunther Artz, his hatchback has a top speed of better than 162mph (260kph), which is 6mph (10kph) better than the coupé.

Another of Gunther Artz's pet obsessions is the Q-car: the wolf dressed up as a little old granny.

This trend started when Artz hid a Porsche Carrera engine under the hood of a 1950s split-window VW Beetle. The whole engine-plus-transmission unit had to be turned 180 degrees to get it inside the wheelbase, and in the end it took up most of the rear seat. The phony Beetle could do better than 137mph (220kph), while Artz had scrupulously kept the outside appearance of the old car exactly as he had found it. Many a BMW, Mercedes or Golf GTi driver was taken in by Artz's little game, and many subsequently added their names to his list of clients.

Gunther Artz executed several replicas of this venomous little Beetle, but he soon encountered an unexpected problem: 1950s vintage Volkswagens have become collector cars and nobody wants to take the blowtorch to them any more. So Artz set about creating his 928S-powered Golf. Since the car's body was too narrow to house the V8 engine, Artz simply sliced it down the middle lengthwise, separated the two halves by 8in (20cm) and proceeded to weld a strip of sheet-metal in the gap. Always faithful to his policy of making his trick cars blend into the scenery, he repainted the whole car an anonymous suburban gray. The whole thing is so meticulously done that you have to line up an ordinary Golf next to the widened 'hot' one before you realize that Artz's creation looks any different. But out on the highway, the 928S Golf casts off its disguise and sets out to hunt (at 155mph [250kph] . . .) the more prestigious denizens of the fast lane.

Another of Gunther Artz's accomplishments is to have transformed a Ferrari 308 GTSi into a convertible. He did away with the roll-bar and installed a comfortable canopy instead. At the same time, Artz trimmed the car in a more stylish manner and painted it – trim and paintwork have never really been Maranello's forte.

In the Artz workshop, the Ferrari 308 GTSi Spyder exchanges its roll-bar for a comfortable soft top. The paintwork and the trim have been reworked at the same time, presumably with a little more attention to detail than they received in the Ferrari factory. Enzo would have every reason to be proud of the result.

ARTZ

Aston Martin

The mutants from Newport Pagnell. In June 1975, Aston Martin seemed to be well and truly a thing of the past: the factory had closed, the staff had been laid off and the machine tools were gathering dust in the deserted workshops.

Aston Martin was already clinically dead when it was bought for £1 million by the American, Peter Sprague. His associate Alan Curtis took on the job of Manager, and slowly Newport Pagnell came back to life once again. The first task was to lure back the necessary staff: most of them had been quickly snapped up by Rolls-Royce. Then Alan Curtis set about improving quality-control on the assembly line, in order to justify a stiff increase in the price of his cars. An Aston Martin was no longer to be just a more refined Jaguar, but a more sporty Rolls-Royce. Finally, in an effort to update Aston Martin's image, Curtis and Sprague unveiled, toward the end of 1976, the prototype of the spectacular Lagonda saloon.

In 1978, for the very first time since it was founded way back in 1913, the firm of Aston Martin recorded a profit. This spurred Alan Curtis to give his go-ahead for the construction of a prototype of the car that was to symbolize Aston Martin's resurrection.

The new car was the Bulldog, Aston Martin's first mid-engined small saloon, presented to the public in April 1980.

The styling of the Bulldog was the work of William Towns, who had designed the entire range of Aston Martin models since the DB6. Towns had reworked, in a far more radical vein, the lines that he had tried out in 1976 on the Lagonda saloon.

With its flattish plane surfaces and sharp ridges, the Bulldog seemed to have been shaped out of a solid block with an axe. The bodywork looked as though the sheet-metal had been shaped by the 'fold-along-the-dotted-line' method.

Yet William Towns had managed to avoid the usual pitfalls of small, mid-engined saloons.

The Bulldog seems designed to forge ahead with all the brutality of a wedge being driven in by a sledge-hammer. And it does pack a heavy punch! An Aston Martin V8, egged on by two Garrett turbos, the whole package develops more than 600bhp. The Bulldog's top speed is theoretically in excess of 199mph (320kph). The little flap just under the windshield hides the control handle that opens the doors.

The Bulldog is more typically Giugiaro than Giugiaro could ever manage . . . with his 'folded cardboard' style, the English stylist William Towns manages to beat his Italian colleague at his own game.

The door of the Bulldog incorporates quite a large chunk of the lower body, in order to provide much easier access to the seats. The gull-wing doors are raised by hydraulic rams, coupled to an electric pump. The Bulldog's interior, classically upholstered in dark leather, is much more reassuring than the car's exterior. A flap on the front hood drops down to reveal a battery of five headlamps.

These cars usually allow about as much visibility as a minisubmarine, and are not much easier to get in and out of either. The windows of the driver's compartment encroached well and truly on to the engine compartment. The doors were hinged in the roof, and when they opened they took with them a large slice of the rocker panel to allow for easier access to the interior.

The Bulldog seemed to have been designed to carve its way through the air with all the subtlety of a wedge being pounded in by a sledge-hammer. And the comparison is valid: the rear end housed a whole strike-force – a 5.34-liter Aston Martin V8 powerplant that had been given extra boost by the addition of two Garrett turbo-chargers.

The specialists rated the Bulldog's power at about 600bhp, but the manufacturer as usual refused to disclose any precise figures. They didn't really need to: it was easy enough to figure out that the rear-axle ratio gave 31mph (50kph) per 1000rpm. Therefore the maximum revs of 6500rpm would turn out a theoretical top speed of . . . 202mph (325kph).

The story went around that the Bulldog in fact owed its existence to one of Aston Martin's richer clients who had offered to finance on his own the construction of a prototype. And you get no marks for guessing that the rich car-lover hailed from the Middle East somewhere. He is said to have put down a very sizeable deposit (£100,000 – or so the story goes) but never showed up to take delivery. It seems that his family, rather worried about his spending habits, had obliged him to engage a legal adviser.

The other mutant to come out of Newport Pagnell was the Lagonda saloon that was presented at the London Motor Show in 1976. It stirred up the passions of British car enthusiasts and some

When the Aston Martin Lagonda was unveiled in 1976 it provoked a great deal of comment from press pundits and car enthusiasts alike. People were simply not used to associating the name of Aston Martin (or the name Lagonda, for that matter) with a saloon of such 'outrageous' lines. And to make things worse, the Lagonda had a futuristic dashboard with touch-sensitive buttons and digital instrumentation displays. In the end, honor was saved; the Lagonda found a steady clientele in the Persian Gulf.

considered the Lagonda to be quite revolutionary. But the old-guard Aston Martin fanatics grumbled bitterly about the new saloon. They said that it was no more than a 'pump to bring in the petro-dollars,' or an 'emir's special.'

As it turned out, both sides were wrong.

William Towns's latest toy was more spectacular than it was revolutionary. This was made abundantly clear if you compared the car to the Lamborghini Espada that had come on the scene eight years earlier. English motoring writer L J K Setright rather viciously compared the new Lagonda to 'a Cadillac Seville that is trying hard to look like a Triumph TR7.' Today, the Lagonda is

more frequently likened to a stretched Volvo 760 with a phony radiator grille stuck on the front.

The fanatical old guard was just as mistaken. Underneath a body that was as striking as a straight left from Muhammad Ali, the Lagonda still remained quite faithful to the traditional qualities of all Aston Martins. Despite its weight of 2½ tons, the saloon proved able to negotiate one corner after another with all the grace and agility of a DB6. It could get to 62mph (100kph) in less than 8 seconds and boasted a top speed of more than 137mph (220kph) – with all the smoothness of a jet cruising at 30,000ft (9144m).

The only really futuristic aspect of the Lagonda (the near future, of course) was its dashboard. This was the very first production car to provide complete digital instrumentation readout. Indeed, the dashboard thoroughly deserved its name: it was a vast black panel where the digital figures lit up in red. It was mounted like a spaceship's radar screen, just above a control panel covered with rows of touch-sensitive buttons.

This rather avant-garde feature was in marked contrast to the Olde-England style – Connolly leather and knotty walnut – in which the rest of the car's interior was fitted out. This futuristic touch added to a traditional interior was somewhat reminiscent of Barbarella's luxurious spaceship.

Auburn

Play it again, Sam! This is the car that you were supposed to drive away from the church in, hand in hand and covered in confetti, toward that lovely technicolor sunset of your dreams.

Half a century later, we're into the remakes. We're doing it all over again but with an entirely different cast. Instead of the 8-cylinder supercharged Lycoming, the leading role is taken by a V8 Ford with automatic transmission. The Director is no longer the Auburn-Cord-Duesenberg Corporation but the Pasadena-based California Custom Coach Company (CCC). Luckily, most of the script has been kept as it was. The body is still made up of a long airplane fuselage with a tiny cockpit on top and four teardrop-shaped wings stuck on the corners. The chromed exhaust pipes still stick out of the hood like those rattle snakes that appear in the film *Raiders of the Lost Ark* – an alarming sight!

About 500 of the Auburn 851/852 speedsters were built during 1935 and 1936. This kind of body style had become one of Auburn's specialties since control of the firm had been taken over by the flamboyant Erret Lobban Cord, who had also managed to get his hands on Duesenberg.

In 1934, Auburn, which had until then weathered the economic crisis without undue difficulty, suddenly found itself in financial trouble. So Cord decided to dispatch Duesenberg's chief stylist, Gordon Buehrig, to help out; and with him went August Duesenberg himself.

Buehrig designed a set of new bodies for 1935. As finance was still a bit tight, he was told to exercise his talents in the direction of the mass-production models – coupés and saloons. As for the speedster, which was more of a prestige symbol than a moneymaker, he contented himself with several minor modifications to the 1934 model: he elongated the point at the rear, streamlined the fenders and gave the speedster a new 1935 radiator grille.

For his part, August Duesenberg adapted a centrifugal supercharger to the quiet 8-cylinder

The 876 phaeton bearing the label of California Custom Coach Inc can be seen here posing in front of the former Packard dealership in Pasadena that was refurbished to become CCC's headquarters. Just like in the good old days, the door handles don't seem to want to stay straight, even for as long as it takes to snap a photo.

The etched-glass wind-deflectors are just one of the period accessories faithfully reproduced by CCC.

816

side-valve Lycoming engine. That boosted its power-rating from 115 to 150hp and gave it a satisfying musical whistle into the bargain. The 'blower' was also to be the pretext for adding those superbly decorative exhaust pipes.

The new Auburn speedster was an immediate hit among the inhabitants of Beverly Hills.

Almost without realizing what he was doing, Buehrig had turned out an absolute masterpiece. The jet-set had never seen anything like it; such a generous deployment of pressed steel and all to transport two people and their golf bags . . .

The price tag on the Auburn was $2300, which made it as expensive as a Cadillac saloon, but it cost even more than that to manufacture. The speedster did nothing at all to help Auburn get back on its feet financially, and the firm went broke at the end of 1936.

Forty years went by. And the solid gold planet of Beverly Hills had changed very little. Then two old stagers from the Hollywood studios burst upon the scene: Cecil Gold and Ray Oja. These two had been dreaming about the Auburn speedster. Then one of their friends offered to make a couple of replicas of the fabulous machine. Gold and Oja in fact ordered four of the cars, but it didn't take them long to realize that they were never going to set eyes on their 'Auburns' unless they took charge of the operation themselves. So there, in the quiet little city of Pasadena, resting sleepily in the shade of its palm trees, Gold and Oja founded California Custom Coach Inc. They set up shop in an old Packard dealership that had managed to retain its old-fashioned 1930s décor. And in this period setting, they were soon operating a very modern and dynamic enterprise.

The cars mirrored this blend of old and new: their 1930s bodywork subtly concealed a Ford V8 engine. Not only that but it could also come with an optional turbo-charger, which would have caused Augie Duesenberg's eyes to light up. Pretty soon, a four-seater phaeton version came along to join the classic two-seater speedster.

And last but not least, Gold and Oja were not to make the same mistake that Auburn had made: the price tag on their cars varies according to the customer's specifications, but it is rarely less than $100,000.

People say that Pasadena is a city full of old ladies who have come to end their days relaxing in the shade of the palm trees, and living on the millions amassed by their late husbands before they were struck down by a heart attack. The grandest of these old ladies is without doubt the replica of the Auburn speedster put together by Cecil Gold and Ray Oja. Don't be surprised if their names sound more at home among the credits of a blockbuster movie – they are both old stagers from the Hollywood studios. But today they're in the business of turning out remakes: remakes of the more successful prewar cars, like the Auburn speedster.

B+B

B+B=MC^2. When you live in a palace that looks like a reconstruction of the Versailles Grand Trianon in the middle of the desert, you could be forgiven for finding the finish and the fittings of a Porsche or a Mercedes somewhat austere.

Both the name and the lines of the B+B CW 311 are reminiscent of the famous experimental Mercedes C111s. But the CW 311 is in fact the creation of only one man, Eberhard Schulz, who was at the time working for Porsche. This impressive sports car presented in 1978 is, after the withdrawal of the BMW M1, the only German car to rival the small Italian saloons, produced by Ferrari or Lamborghini. The CW 311 is 100 percent German. Its suspension and brakes come out of the Porsche 928. It has borrowed its 6.9-liter engine from the Mercedes 600 and 450 SEL 6.9 models. And it shares a ZF gearbox with the De Tomaso Pantera. The CW's fiberglass bodywork covers a tubular chassis. The car has several ingenious features: the immense hexagonal windshield is absolutely flat, and the Mercedes V8 valve-covers are left exposed to allow them more height.

Gray velvet and black plastic make for a rather spartan car interior when the telephones at home are all gold plated.

Luckily, you can always fall back on B+B. In this case, B+B stands for Buchmann and Buchmann. For the last 15 years, the Buchmann brothers from Frankfurt have been taking Porsches and Mercedes, and giving them that little touch of extravagance that makes all the difference.

Gold-plated fittings, color television, digital display instrumentation, the most explosive hi-fi music system on the market, and ultra-toughened armor-plating (if considered necessary). These are just a few of the features that have made B+B cars such a success.

And yet with the CW 311, the Buchmanns were able to achieve a breakthrough into a brand new dimension.

This very impressive mid-engined small saloon was débuted in 1978. It was built around the 6.9-liter V8 engine that powered the Mercedes 600. The superb 5-speed ZF gearbox was borrowed from the De Tomaso Pantera, and the brakes and suspension system were lifted from the Porsche 928.

Clearly this was not the sort of car that you could put together in your own backyard. B+B boasted a top speed in excess of 186mph (300kph), and they said that the CW 311 could reach 62mph (100kph) from a standing start in under 5 seconds. But to get all this you had to fork out close to a million French francs.

The bodywork was fiberglass, covering a tubular chassis. With its compact styling, which was extremely distinctive, the CW 311's lines were a pleasant reminder of the famous Mercedes C 111 experimental cars. All the more so as Daimler-Benz, as a special favor, had authorized B+B to add the famous three-pointed star to the front of the hood.

The CW 311 also includes several very practical features. The gigantic hexagonal windshield was absolutely flat, which made its fabrication much easier. There was only one external rear-view mirror, stuck on the roof like a periscope, and the driver had to look up at it through a skylight.

In reality, B+B had played only a minor role in the conception of the CW 311. The creative genius behind it was really a man named Eberhard Schulz. Schulz had built the prototype car all alone in his garage before going to see B+B.

At that stage, Schulz was employed by Porsche as a testing engineer and body-stylist. He had put together the CW 311 to give an indication of some of his more radical ideas.

Schulz was soon to set up his very own design office, though, under the name of Isdera (see the chapter devoted to Isdera later in this book). Once he had set up on his own, he took over the CW 311 project, and the new car became the Isdera Imperator. It is still powered by the biggest of the Daimler-Benz V8 range: its slightly reduced engine-capacity (5.6 liters) is more than made up for by two AMG cylinder heads with twin overhead camshafts and four valves per cylinder.

F CW 311

F CW 311

AMG

F-CW 311

'Come for a ride in my Porsche. It's even got a TV . . .'

dashboard look more like the mixing console of a sound-recording studio. As there was still a little space left, the makers added a color television. It must have been intended to help pass the time while the car was stuck in traffic jams rather than to relieve the monotonous boredom of the highways – after all, Curaçao's little stretch of highway is all of 1.86m (3km) long . . .

The front of the car has been restyled, following the fashion trend that started in the United States, to incorporate the retractable headlamps of the Porsche 928.

To indulge in this little exercise in fantasy cost the B+B's buyer a quarter of a million German marks, 10 years ago. Since then, the Buchmanns have built several replicas. Some of them have a hard top incorporating two removable sections, rather like the 'T-roof' on a Corvette. Of course

Ten years after the CW 311 was first introduced, they are still being made, but the workshop turns them out with painstaking slowness (one by one) for the privileged few.

Casino, palm trees and a revolver in the glove-box – this Porsche 911 Turbo Targa sweeps you off into the fantasy world of James Bond and his glamorous friends.

It was ordered from B+B in 1977 by a wealthy casino-owner from Curaçao in the West Indies. There's a Magnum revolver hidden in a secret compartment; that packs a much bigger punch than a giant bottle of champagne ever would. You open the lethal compartment by pressing one of the little buttons on the console of the Recaro seat, but as far as can be ascertained, the seat itself does not eject out.

A very complete hi-fi system up front makes the

they were also given an instrument panel featuring the DINFOS digital display system that was one of B+B's inventions.

There was one little detail on the early 928s to come off the production line that didn't manage to escape the eagle eyes of Porsche enthusiasts: included in their chassis number was the code number that had been adopted by Porsche to designate a coupé model. So the Porsche fans started asking themselves why Porsche bothered to include the coupé code when the coupé was the only version of the 928 being made?

There could, of course, (or so they told themselves) be only one reason: the men at Porsche must be planning another version . . .

What could the factory have in mind? It was fairly unlikely that they would build a saloon, and a station wagon or hatchback was even more improbable despite the precedent already set by the Artz.

So there was only one solution: Porsche must build a 928 convertible. And 928-lovers started hopping up and down with excitement.

All their ardent hopes were soon to be shattered: three years later, the mysterious code number had vanished from the chassis number and the little 928 was condemned to remain a coupé for the rest of its days.

It is this sort of frustration that stimulates people like the Buchmann brothers to greater things, more so as B+B were always on the lookout for openings that had been overlooked by the major German car manufacturers.

The Buchmanns' first reaction was to present, at the 1979 Frankfurt Motor Show, a 928 Targa that displayed one rather ingenious particularity. It had a beam running lengthways between the roll-bar and the windshield, housing a hi-fi stereo system. In addition to this, a largish front skirt was installed to 'harden' intentionally the rather vapid lines of the original 928.

B+B went one better at the 1981 Geneva Salon. This time they put on show a true convertible whose soft top, once lowered, disappeared completely from view underneath a special metal cover. Obviously, B+B had sacrificed the back seats, but that meant all the more room for any luggage that was being carried.

They had also redesigned the rear of the car to make it follow the lines of the quarter-panels. This was without doubt a styling success, but it meant that the trunk ended up not much bigger than the glove compartment.

In 1981 B+B received a very special order. They were asked to transform a Mercedes 600 according to the specifications of a Middle East oil king who dreamed nostalgically of those big parade Mercedes of the 1930s.

The 600 had been launched in 1963 and was supposed to be Daimler-Benz's answer to the Bugatti Royale. In the D-B catalogue one reads that the 600 was 'specially constructed for Chiefs of State and other leading personages charged with fulfilling important official functions.' The message struck home: the 600 found clients aplenty, ranging from the Pope to Chairman Mao, not forgetting Idi Amin Dada. But the two German republics declined to take up the offer: the enormous Mercedes would awaken too many embarrassing memories in their countries.

B+B is always on the lookout for any opening neglected by the larger German car manufacturers. In 1979, the Frankfurt firm unveiled their 928 Targa, and then in 1981 it was the 928 convertible.

To quote B+B, the aerodynamic front spoiler was intended to give the physiognomy of the Porsche 928 a 'more virile' look. Note the use of the roof-beam.

The 600 remained in production for 17 years with only minor modifications. And yet only 2677 of them were built in all of that time. In 1980 Mercedes clients were informed that the model was to be discontinued at the end of the year.

So an eminent emir quickly placed an order for a whole fleet of Mercedes 600s, to transport both him and his entourage. But he wanted his own limousine to stand out from all the rest.

For the front of his car, the emir wanted B+B to draw their inspiration from a 1936 model 500 K roadster that had been sold in 1979 for more than $400,000 (in fact, the very same car that was to inspire Franco Sbarro). The emir also specified running boards long enough to accommodate at least two bodyguards along each side.

B+B's famous virtuoso metal-worker, the Spaniard Manuel Melero, was commissioned to give the two front fenders their shapely curve. The displaced front axle also meant that the chassis, the steering and the hydraulic system all had to be modified too. A magnificent pair of headlamps copied from the enormous prewar Zeiss design, and specially designed bumpers, completed the front end.

B+B's transformation of a
Mercedes 600, styled exclusively
for a Middle East sheik.

Bertone

Together, they were betting on the future. At the 1965 Turin Motor Show, Lamborghini had put on display an experimental chassis with a sideways-mounted engine at the rear. As soon as he caught sight of it, Nuccio Bertone was heard to exclaim: 'That's the chassis I've always dreamed of. I must have it!'

Six months later, at the Geneva Salon, the Lamborghini Miura made its début. Indeed, throughout his career, Nuccio Bertone was always falling in 'love at first sight' like this. And on two of these occasions, he ended up hiring obscure novice stylists called Giorgio Giugiaro (who was only 19 years old at the time) and Marcello Gandini (who had just reached the age of 21).

And ever since the Miura, every time Bertone and Lamborghini came together, they ended up producing a masterpiece.

At the 1967 Geneva Salon, they unveiled the Marzal. Ferruccio Lamborghini had in mind to turn it into a four-seater model (the future Espada). But he also wanted to put on show a spectacular machine that would make the cover of all the glossy motoring magazines. He was not going to be disappointed.

With the Marzal, Bertone had proved that he could work his magic just as well on a four-seater saloon as on its smaller sister.

The rear-engined Marzal was powered by a sideways-mounted 6-cylinder engine that was simply the Miura's V12 cut in half. The doors were hinged in the roof panel to provide easier access to the rear seats, but Bertone was undoubtedly extremely aware that they would look attractive too. They were almost totally glassed-in, like a helicopter's doors. From the side, the body took the form of an elongated hexagon. The hexagon motif was repeated on the dashboard and also on the vent-paneling of the engine cover, which as a result ended up looking rather like an enormous beehive.

The Marzal made a second appearance on the occasion of the Monaco Grand Prix, where the car did an opening lap of the circuit with Prince

This photo shows quite clearly the hexagonal shape that is the basis of the Marzal's body-styling. The hexagon motif is repeated on the dashboard and again on the rear engine cover, which looks like a gigantic beehive. Bertone presented the Marzal at the 1967 Geneva Show, managing the same *coup de théâtre* that he had brought off with the Miura a year earlier. The Marzal still has a place of honor in Bertone's private museum.

The doors on the Marzal were completely glassed-in; like the doors of a helicopter.

Even all these years later, it is hard to imagine more radical styling than that of the Stratos in 1970.

Rainier at the wheel. It was the first time the Marzal had been out on the road. Until then it had only appeared on display stands, and the engineers found they had to load an anvil into the trunk to ensure stability.

Back in 1946, Pinin Farina had brought the automobile into the jet-age. At the Turin Motor Show of 1970, Bertone finally launched the motorcar into the space-age. He accomplished this *tour de force* with the Stratos – the earthly equivalent of an Apollo space capsule.

Nowadays it is still difficult to imagine more radical body-lines than the ones that were shown off on the Stratos in 1970. The designer had managed to refine the wedge shape to its absolute essentials.

With the Stratos, stylist Marcello Gandini, for his part, had pushed to an extreme limit the innovations tried out on the memorable Carabo the year before.

The driving compartment of the Stratos was sunk down inside the bodywork. To climb inside, the driver had to raise up the windshield section which, just as on the late-lamented Isetta, took the steering-wheel up with it. The two small side-windows (one is tempted to call them portholes) were all that was left of the glassed-in helicopter doors on the Marzal. And the best that these openings could offer the half-prone occupants of the Stratos was an unbeatable view of passing hub-caps.

The vent-panels on the engine compartment formed a decorative motif that seemed to have been chiseled into the pressed steel of the body.

You climb inside the Stratos by lifting the windshield, which takes the steering-wheel up with it. The front 'hood' which is left behind is really nothing more than a step for the driver. Contrary to appearances, the Stratos was not a static *objet d'art* at all. A Lancia Fulvia engine and transmission unit made sure it had 'go' as well as 'show,' thus preparing the way for the future Lancia Stratos with its Ferrari engine.

BERTONE

And as with the Carabo, the air intakes for the radiator were repeated in a mirror-image motif on the lower half of the main body-panel. This quest for symmetry of body line is reminiscent of Pinin Farina's work on the Modulo, which was unveiled at about the same time.

Yet the Stratos had another surprise up its sleeve: it wasn't a piece of static sculpture at all! The engine and transmission unit borrowed from the Lancia Fulvia and mounted at the rear allowed the Stratos to move quite convincingly, and the denizens of Turin soon got quite used to seeing this pressed metal flatfish driving around the streets of their fair city. Of course they had been conditioned to these strange sights: only a year before they had been confronted with a fabulous clockwork insect called the Carabo.

Lamborghini's most creative phase was the period between 1965 and 1975. During this almost continuous spurt of creative energy, Bertone managed not only to match the frenzied production of models maintained by Lamborghini, but once or twice he even managed to get ahead of his employer.

So it was, as early as 1971, that the Miura was superseded at the very height of its success by the Countach. Bertone had chosen to dress this prototype with such a sensational body that Lamborghini really had little choice of action: they would just have to set up a full production line.

And in 1974, when production of the new Urraco had hardly even got under way, Bertone was already taking the wraps off the model that would, to all intents and purposes, be the Urraco's successor – the Bravo.

The Bravo, with its sideways-mounted, 3-liter twin overhead camshaft engine, had been

In 1974, Lamborghini's production run for Bertone's little Urraco had only just got under way when Bertone, as impatient as ever, was already busy unveiling its effective successor: the Bravo. The new car was based on the Urraco P 300 and had a 3-liter twin overhead camshaft V8 engine mounted sideways. The Bravo represents the high-point in Bertone's 'space-capsule' period: it is a less dramatic but more practical car than the Stratos. Note the window panels that come together outside the door pillars, effectively concealing them. This fabulous little machine was sadly the only one of its kind ever built.

The compact lines of the Bravo are accentuated by the foil-counterfoil effect generated by the use of matching air-vents for the front radiator and the rear engine compartment.

BRAVO

BERTONE

The Lancia Sibilo: Bertone without Lamborghini but with more than a dash of the Bravo and the Jalpa. Notice the strange absence of windows: they have simply been replaced by synthetic body-panels, made transparent in those places where windows would normally be. In the Sibilo, one can already discern traces of the Athon (opposite).

designed using the Urraco P 300 as a starting-point. And then the pretty little Urraco itself started to throw a spanner in the works.

The Urraco had been introduced in 1970, with a haste that was rather typical of Lamborghini, and the car really only went into full production in 1973. Meanwhile, the gas crisis and all the consequences that it engendered had covered the world in a pall of gloom. The little Lamborghini had been designed with the American market in mind, but by the time it reached the other side of the Atlantic the party was all over . . .

Just about then, Ferruccio Lamborghini decided to retire and went off to prune his grape-vines on the slopes of Lake Trasimeno. He had sold out to some Swiss businessmen. So it was that only the one Bravo was ever built. But for many years afterward, every time that things looked a bit brighter for Lamborghini, the question of a Bravo production run kept cropping up on the company's agenda.

It is said that there is more to life than simple survival. And for quite some time Lamborghini did just that. One can only hope that new owners, car giant Chrysler, will re-create those glorious times 15 or 20 years ago when the firm was possessed by a frantic thirst for life.

As for Bertone, his recent designs show a kind of nostalgic yearning. A good example is the Lancia Sibilo, which looks a lot like a Bravo with the Jalpa's wheel arches added. Yet Bertone has added one interesting innovation: strictly speaking, the car has no windows. The car's body-panels, which are constructed out of synthetic material, are simply made to be transparent where the windows would usually be. The Sibilo bears some resemblance to Bertone's later styling creation, the Athon.

With his more recent styling creations, like the Lamborghini Athon (left) or the Alfa Romeo Delfino (right), Bertone evokes a world where electronics has left its mark on everything. The Athon looks like a gigantic Walkman with the driver wearing the earphones. With the Delfino, it is the electronic-looking dashboard that sets the tone for the whole of the styling.

In 1980, Bertone designed his Athon around a Lamborghini chassis in order to lend his support to 'a great name in motoring history' that he did not wish to see disappear. The name Athon refers to 'the force hidden behind the sun' of Egyptian mythology.

Bertone's Athon was presented at the Turin Motor Show in 1980. It attracted extremely unfavorable press reviews, mainly because of its 'ugliness.' Comparing the car with the Alfa Romeo Delfino gives a better idea of what the designer originally had in mind.

The first thing to notice is that the body and the dashboard are executed in exactly the same style. But while with an American car of the 1950s era the dashboard always takes its cue from the rest of the body-lines, with the Delfino the body-styling seems to draw its inspiration from the instrument panel. The body is styled to resemble some enormous piece of electronic apparatus.

The taillights are as discreet as the lights on a hi-fi music system. The covers on the air filters look like big touch-sensitive control buttons. And the whole body looks like the molded plastic casing of a radio or television set.

Bertone swept us off into an electronic science-fiction universe. Or, if you prefer, the Athon looks rather like a giant Walkman, with the driver wearing the earphones.

This evolution toward the electronic look is quite a logical styling development. For the last 50 years, the automobile has had no real style of its own. Starting in the 1930s, stylists drew most of their inspiration from the world of aeronautics. Then at the end of the 1960s, the conquest of space provided a new source of styling inspiration; wedge-shaped forms, like space-capsules, were all the rage.

What Bertone is telling us with the Delfino is that, in a world dominated by electronics, these very same 'black boxes' will serve as models for the other objects that our civilization generates. He may be wrong, but once again, Bertone is betting on the future.

BERTONE
delfino

Clenet

The Clenet takes us right back to the 1930s when the Hollywood razzmatazz was in full swing, back to the days when the Marx Brothers' Mercedes used to race down Sunset Boulevard neck and neck with Al Jolson's Duesenberg.

The Clenet is the kind of car that Clark Gable (or Gary Cooper) would have gone out and bought as soon as he found out that Gary Cooper (or Clark Gable) had got one.

At first sight, the Clenet looks like something out of a Tex Avery cartoon: the one that shows the snobbish young playboy poser with his cigarette-holder and his droopy little moustache. The hood of his car is so long that it takes almost as long as a goods train to drive across the screen.

It's a fact that the hood of the Clenet takes up a good three-quarters of its wheelbase, rather like the body of a Mercedes SSK or a Duesenberg SSJ. Its driver finds himself in much the same situation as if he was trying to drive a Cadillac from the back seat!

And yet the Clenet was quite seriously expected to make money.

When Frenchman Alain Clenet arrived in the United States in 1965, he was only 21 years old. First of all he went to work in Detroit, but by 1975 he had set up his own company in Santa Barbara, out on the very edge of the urban galaxy of Los Angeles, California.

It was there that Clenet started building the automobile that was to bear his name. The starting point for the Clenet (as if it wasn't quite obvious) was the little English MGB. But Clenet had to stretch the chassis quite a bit forward to accommodate a Lincoln V8 engine with its 4-speed automatic transmission.

Clenet himself (he did, after all, have a designer's diploma) undertook the car's styling, and he turned out a machine that looked just like one of those automotive superstars of the 1930s. Clenet's stated aim was to arrive at a style synthesis of a whole motoring era, rather than to simply turn out a replica of a particular model. In the end, the fenders are reminiscent of the Bugatti Royale, the exposed exhaust pipes hark back to the Duesenberg SJ, and the Clenet's general proportions seem to have been inspired by the Mercedes SSK. But the car's radiator grille is pure, unadulterated Clenet: no car manufacturer had produced anything quite like it back in the 1930s.

The Clenet, or so its creator liked to insist, is in fact a totally modern car. The body just happens to look old fashioned: for Alain Clenet it is simply the kind of styling that is best suited to a thoroughly luxurious motorcar. Clenet was often heard to remark that the most expensive objects are frequently styled in a very traditional manner. Indeed, the interior styling of prestige automobiles is almost always executed in traditional materials such as wood, leather and cloth. Therefore, reasoned Clenet, why not apply this same respect for traditional design to the styling of the car as well?

In any case, Clenet's pastiche (or re-creation) of a 1930s supercar was executed with a lot of flair and a superb sense of proportion. You only have to compare the Clenet with the Excalibur, its only rival when it first appeared, to see quite clearly all the pitfalls that the Frenchman managed to avoid when styling the car.

Clenet had another card up his sleeve too: his swinging lifestyle brought him into everyday contact with his potential clientele. His young playboy look was the best advertisement imaginable for his car. His intimate knowledge of the jet-set meant that he immediately understood just what they wanted. And he signed up his most faithful customers between two chukkas of a polo match.

So the Clenet was very carefully calculated to appeal to the cupidity of the snobbish Tex Avery playboy, with all his usual mannerisms. At the sight of the Frenchman's gleaming creation, the young blade's eyes were supposed to pop out like a pair of telescopes, his hair would stand up on end, and he would jump up and down unable to contain himself with excitement.

Sitting behind the wheel of a Clenet, you find yourself in much the same position as if you were driving a Cadillac from the back seat.

The Clenet is not a replica of any car that ever really existed. It is more a synthesis of several superstars from the golden age of motoring: its front fenders are reminiscent of the Bugatti Royale, its exposed exhaust pipes are borrowed from the Duesenberg SJ, and its body proportions seem inspired by the Mercedes SSK. But the radiator grille is all Clenet's own work. The car is based on the English MGB chassis, stretched forward in order to accommodate a Lincoln V8 engine with automatic transmission.

CALIFORNIA
CLENET

CHEVROLE

Giugiaro

He was probably the most influential designer of his time. So much so that in the future, our present day may well be referred to as the age of Giorgio Giugiaro.

Man has already seen the Age of the Cathedrals just as he has lived through the century of Louis XIV. And if sociologist Roland Barthes is right, then the automobile is the 'modern day's equivalent of the cathedral.' Surely then, the man who has left his mark so indelibly on the modern automobile deserves, just as much as Louis XIV, to give his name to his century. And Giugiaro's influence does not stop at automobiles: if one day you notice an uncanny resemblance between your camera, the family sewing machine and your eldest daughter's little VW Golf, then it's probably because all three objects were designed by Giorgio Giugiaro.

Schoolboys in the year 2500 or even 3000, yawning with boredom just as we did, will probably have to learn about Giorgio Giugiaro. You can just see them now, copying out in their little notebooks (which will really be microchip touch-screens of course . . .) summaries like this:

Giorgio Giugiaro was born on 17 August 1938 in the little town of Garessio, situated about 62m (100km) from Turin. His family tree already boasted several generations of artists, painters, sculptors and musicians. Little Giorgio soon followed in their footsteps, enrolling in the Academy of Fine Arts at Turin. Giugiaro held his first exhibition in 1955, at the age of 17, and as a result was immediately employed by Fiat as a junior stylist for the firm. It was there at Fiat that Giugiaro learned his trade, under the watchful eye of the famous Dante Giacosa.

These years spent working for a major car manufacturer proved to be very valuable for the rest of his career. Giugiaro readily admits today that one of the most important things he learned at Fiat was that 'when designing an object, one should never lose sight of the function it is supposed to perform, or indeed the fabrication processes it will require. It seems to me that this fundamental truth holds good for the design of a motorcar just as it does for any other object.'

Giugiaro put these very same principles into practice in one of his more recent prototypes: the Gabbiano, which is based on the normal wheelbase of a Renault II.

In spite of its appearance, the gull-wing doors are not (for once . . .) a desperate eye-catcher added by a body designer who has simply run out of true inspiration. They are designed to fulfill two very specific needs.

The first is to facilitate access to the vehicle when it is parked in a very narrow space, which is more and more the rule in countries where there is now one motorcar for every three or four inhabitants. And by shifting the pivotal axis to the center of the roof panel, Giugiaro has reduced as far as possible the side clearance needed to open the door. This is one advantage that is certainly not offered by a car like the De Lorean, where the door hinge has been located on the outer edge of the roof panel.

The second reason for the gull-wing doors is that the Gabbiano is a streamlined coupé that has been based on a Renault II. Because of the lowered roof, only a door that lifts up can provide easy access to the rear seats.

It is worth noting, in passing, that doors that lift up are quite an old idea. They are yet another of the many elements of automobile design that have been inspired, over the last 50 years, by the world of aeronautics. At one stage, Jean Bugatti considered using the technique on his 57 S Atlantic coupé. And the idea was taken up again after the war by Mercedes and used on the 300 SL coupé. But Mercedes chose this solution for very precise technical reasons: the light tubular chassis that they had chosen to use would have been greatly weakened if the door-openings went down to the 'normal' level of the rocker panel. And that left only one other way of getting into the car: the driver would have to climb in from the top.

The 300 SL coupés raced at Le Mans, but soon

The Gabbiano; the Renault II according to Giugiaro. In recent times, designers have been perhaps a little too free with doors that hinge in the roof. With the Gabbiano, they seem justified for once. They were designed to make for easier access to the rear seats, despite the low roof of this streamlined coupé. You also had to be able to open the car's door in the confined spaces of today's parking lots.

PIRELLI

afterward cars with gull-wing doors were officially banned from racing there. The reason given was very simple: if a car with doors hinging in the roof were to roll over, then the driver would end up trapped inside. So it was that the Ford GT40, which was originally intended to have gull-wings, eventually had to fall back on doors that opened by the usual manner.

The way the interior of the Gabbiano is trimmed demonstrates Giugiaro's desire to present a 'complete' car, designed as an integrated whole and not just conceived as an impressive outer shell. For Giugiaro, an automobile should constitute a unified ensemble with all the elements working together in complete harmony. When the Italian presents a project, he has already studied every last detail. This is one of the reasons why he takes very unkindly to car manufacturers who see fit to modify his design without first consulting him. Certainly, his business sense makes Giugiaro realize that in the final analysis the customer is always right, but his artistic sense (or is it instinct?) violently objects to this.

Giorgio Giugiaro has good commercial sense, in spite of being a scrupulous and very demanding artist. So it is that the angular little Golf was supposed to have square headlamps, the rear uprights on the Lancia Delta were to have been much slimmer, and the trunk of the Alfasud was to have opened in a different way. As far as Giugiaro is concerned, these modifications betray his original conception of the car in question.

Now that Giugiaro is famous, he can defend his original design from a position of strength. If he doesn't like the way a manufacturer modifies it, then he refuses to allow his name to be used in any advertising for the car. Giugiaro resorted to this tactic recently with one of the major car manufacturers; the firm took it upon itself to extend the main section of the body downward by 1.2in (3cm) without consulting the stylist. Giugiaro's position certainly gives the manufacturers food for thought: they know that the GG signature on a car can have the same effect on sales as a top couturier's label attached to an expensive cocktail dress.

And Giugiaro learned very quickly just what his signature was worth.

The Orca: one of Giorgio Giugiaro's more recent creations. Here, the designer was trying to demonstrate that a standard 4-door saloon can be both roomy and nicely streamlined. The usual drag coefficient for a car in this class is between 0.32 and 0.35. Giugiaro has managed to keep the Orca's under 0.25 and yet the provision of passenger space is far more roomy and comfortable than average.

He made his real styling début when he met Bertone for the first time at the Turin Motor Show. He showed Bertone a few sketches from his portfolio and was hired on the spot. This was a real achievement for someone so young.

His career at Bertone's began with a flourish: the Alfa Romeo 2600 coupé, which has remained one of Alfa's all-time classics. Other very striking Giugiaro creations were to follow, and in a surprisingly short space of time. He worked with chassis made by Fiat, Alfa Romeo and Iso, not to mention the very beautiful Ferrari 250 GT that went on show at the Geneva Salon in 1971.

The interior and (below) the dashboard of the Gabbiano: Giorgio Giugiaro's car designs extend to the last detail.

Giugiaro soon felt a little frustrated at being just another of Bertone's anonymous designers. At the end of 1965, he abruptly left Bertone to go to work for another styling studio, Ghia. Here he produced his masterpieces: the De Tomaso Mangusta and the Maserati Ghibli.

Giugiaro only stayed with Ghia two years, leaving in 1968 to found the Ital Design studio.

This new phase in Giugiaro's life obviously called for a new style, and the first expression of it to be unveiled was the Alfa Romeo Iguana. This car heralded the birth of the famous Giugiaro style that was to find worldwide expression.

ITAL DESIGN

Isdera

It has to be a speedster. Nothing else will do. The wind hitting your face makes you think someone has turned a firehose on you full blast. There's nothing but a little wind-deflector in front of you and a head-rest behind: you have about as much protection from the elements as Manfred von Richthofen, flying his bright-red Fokker triplane.

The elements massage you, buffet and squeeze you. It's simply unbelievable how solid air can seem when you're ploughing through it at 87mph (140kph). The motorcycling crowd wave to you as you pass: you're one of the fraternity now.

Behind the wheel of the Isdera Spyder, you are in a position to rediscover certain basic truths that have been forgotten ever since the windshield was invented. This one for example: the world is basically a hostile place, and you have to fight to carve out a path for yourself. But the struggle is worth it – your reward is to regain the forgotten savor of some of the very simple things in life: like the shafts of sunlight filtering through the trees, the scent of freshly cut hay, or the beauty of a narrow country road, winding down a hillside.

Isdera: it sounds a bit like one of those girls' names that a Hamburg docker might choose to have tattooed on his arm. In fact it is an acronym standing for *Ingenieurburo für Styling Design und Racing.* You could be forgiven for thinking that this is one of those trilingual announcements you hear aboard an airplane these days – only the air-hostess has muddled up her notes to make the announcement! Let's face it, Isdera sounds a whole lot more attractive.

The Isdera was the brainchild of a man called Eberhard Schulz. For Schulz, a sports car didn't necessarily have to be a watertight, sound-proofed machine with heating and a hi-fi. He saw it as a vehicle stripped to the bare essentials: not much more than four wheels and an engine – something as functional as a pair of skis. And you don't see many skis with heating and a hi-fi . . .

But simple doesn't necessarily mean rudimentary. If you give a ski more than a passing glance

A sports car that was nothing but a sports car, that was what Eberhard Schulz had always dreamed of building. He made his dream come true with the Isdera Spyder. It is a 1980s-style reincarnation of the famous Porsche 356 speedster of the 1950s.

The Isdera Spyder is basically an open version of Eberhard Schulz's previous creation: the B+B CW 311 coupé (see pp 21-23). Moreover, Schulz was soon to reclaim the CW 311 for his own under the name of Isdera Imperator. As is fitting, the two Isdera models are brothers but sworn enemies too. They have totally opposed personalities. And their natural habitat is completely different too: the coupé feels at home on the highway while the Spyder much prefers the picturesque side-roads.

you will realize that it is a very high-tech object. But it's still no good for anything except skiing. That's the trouble with modern sports cars – they tend to be equipped with all sorts of luxuries, which detract from the essential pleasure of a fast car. Feeling warm or listening to your favorite symphony are examples of such accessory diversions that interfere with that fundamental pleasure of a sports car – driving it.

With some sports cars, the accessory diversions have a tendency to overshadow that fundamental driving pleasure to such an extent that sometimes there seems to be virtually no driving pleasure left. But there's probably little point in giving examples here.

Eberhard Schulz had dreamed for a long time of owning a sports car that was the motoring equivalent of a pair of skis. And Schulz had known for many years what that ideal sports car looked like: it was the Porsche 356 speedster of the 1950s.

The 356 model has doubtless done more for the Porsche mystique than all the other Porsches between them. Its story is a rather strange one. Some cars owe their success to their styling, others to the power unit that is hidden underneath. The Porsche speedster must be the only car in motoring history that became a legend simply because of its windshield!

The curious thing about the speedster was really its absence of windshield. Well, in reality it had a sort of half-windshield, or windshield in embryo.

Now, the usual function of a windshield is to protect the occupants of the vehicle from the wind. Only the speedster's windshield seemed to have been designed to funnel the air stream with increased intensity straight into the driver's face. And this wasn't the only quaint peculiarity of the little Porsche . . .

The speedster's foldback top looked just like your grandmother's umbrella, except that it was a lot less use than an umbrella. The roof canopy was so difficult to put up when it started to rain that most Porsche owners soon learned to do without it altogether. One of them is said to have quipped, 'If it starts to rain, it's a lot faster to stop and put your swimsuit on.'

The speedster's fittings and accessories were pared down to the strict essentials. Its interior was just as spartan as that of the Volkswagen in the days when it was still called the KdF.

The result was that there was very little that could distract the driver from the basic pleasure of driving his 356. He could devote all his attention to the little car's magnificent road-holding. And the engine whining just behind his back gave him the feeling of being relentlessly pursued by an impatient and angry motorcyclist.

That is how the Porsche 356 speedster did more for Ferdinand Porsche's prestige than either the 917 or even the 911 Turbo.

After dreaming for so long about the speedster, Eberhard Schulz finally designed a modernized version of the car and took it along to Porsche for them to see. The Zuffenhausen management hired him as a stylist for the company right there and then.

Schulz learned a great deal while working for Porsche. In particular, he began to appreciate the many and varied resources that the city of Stuttgart and its environs had to offer an automobile manufacturer. You can put together a complete motorcar without ever having to leave town, simply by doing the rounds of firms with names like Bosch, Behr, Recaro and Sikkens. It's all very convenient.

Yet our friend Schulz was not yet satisfied. Porsche had lots of other things on its mind besides his updated speedster (in the event it was only to appear some 10 years later). So Schulz went off to work for the Buchmann brothers who ran the firm of B+B. Working with them, he learned that a small-scale car manufacturer has much more flexibility and can act much more quickly than a big firm. After all, a speedboat can run rings around an ocean liner . . .

Soon Schulz decided that the time had come for him to stand on his own two feet, and he set up the firm of Isdera. Isdera would be to Porsche what Porsche was to Volkswagen.

Schulz built his Isdera Spyder around the engine and transmission unit out of the Golf GTi (or the Audi 80 GTE, which amounts to the same thing). This power-unit was centrally mounted at the rear.

isdera
Spyder 033i
BB-ES 956

BB-ES 956

The Isdera Spyder is available in two different versions: the 033i with engine and transmission out of the VW GTi, or the 035i which is powered by the 5-cylinder 2.2-liter turbo-charged unit out of the Audi Quattro. But whichever version you choose, at 124mph (200kph) or at 155mph (250kph) there's no way that your hair or tie are going to stay in place. Eberhard Schulz obviously realized this, and he came up with the idea of providing every Spyder buyer with a complete set of driver's leathers to match the color-scheme of his new car.

The Isdera's engine had benefited quite a lot from the attention of Doktor-Engineer Schick. The addition of a special camshaft and a synchronized exhaust collector made the little 1.8-liter 4-cylinder engine whine much more musically. Its power rating was now able to reach 140bhp(DIN) at 6100rpm.

As the Spyder weighs less than 1543lb (700kg) with everything included, this engine gives the car as much punch as a prize-fighter who has been fed nothing but good lean meat and raw vegetables. It can get to 62mph (100kph) in under 7 seconds. And as for its top speed, the Isdera has

no trouble at all breaking the 124mph (200kph) mark.

For those who find the 033i Spyder still a bit tame, Schulz also puts out an 035i version which is equipped with an Audi Quattro engine: a turbo-charged 5-cylinder 2.2-liter unit, turning out a full 250bhp(DIN) at 5300rpm. The 035i Spyder can get to the 62mph (100kph) mark in 5 seconds and will do almost 155mph (250kph) once it gets its second wind.

At that speed, the driver feels as though he's sitting on the wing of a Boeing as it reaches takeoff point. Obviously there's little point in driving the car decked in business suit and Brylcream. Eberhard Schulz understood the problem perfectly and decided to offer every Spyder buyer a little extra gift: a complete set of driver's leathers (colored to match his car, naturally . . .) with gloves and helmet thrown in! Driver and car were to wear the same livery, just like a Teutonic knight and his charger.

Dressed in these matching leathers, Schulz seems to say, the proud owner of an Isdera will no longer have to dangle the ignition keys ostentatiously to be immediately recognized as one of the very privileged elite.

Lamborghini

At first sight, a four-wheel-drive Lamborghini off-road vehicle seems about as improbable as a Formula One Rolls-Royce.

The Lamborghini LMA: a metal rhinoceros that can climb a 120-degree slope just as effortlessly as it can make a GTi eat its dust. And if the over-enthusiastic driver happens to go into a corner a bit too fast, then he can always just keep on going into the bush . . . It's hard to imagine anything that could stop this 3-ton machine that is all of 2.19yd (2m) wide and 1.97yd (1.8m) high. The engine in the LMA is more or less the same as the one in the Countach. The independent four-wheel suspension with double wishbones and coil-springs looks as though it has been borrowed from some gigantic Formula One racer. The large gas tank allows you to take off for the next oasis without a care in the world. And those who are still not satisfied can always put in a special order to have their monstrous dune buggy powered by the 7.2-liter Lamborghini V12 speedboat engine!

Who could possibly suspect that the LM, which looks about as graceful as a metal rhinoceros getting ready to charge, hides under its carapace one of the most perfect engineering expressions of the principle of Art for Art's sake: a Lamborghini V12 that is very similar to the powerplant of the fabulous Countach.

The letters LM stand for Lamborghini Mimran. In September 1980, the young (he was 24 at the time) Patrick Mimran became President of Lamborghini. One of his first decisions was to resurrect one of the firm's lesser-known creations: an off-road machine called the Cheetah that was first presented at the Geneva Show in 1977.

The Cheetah was a sort of giant dune buggy powered by a Chrysler V8 engine, and had been produced on order from an American company. The original Cheetah had been shipped across the Atlantic and had long since disappeared without trace. So it was something of a surprise when, at the 1981 Geneva Show, Lamborghini unveiled a new version of the vehicle and christened it the LM001.

The new Lamborghini had been given the same aggressively utilitarian appearance as the Cheetah, and it looked more like a piece of earth-moving equipment than the latest offering from a prestigious high-performance car manufacturer. Moreover, the LM001 was available in a civilian or military version. Hard-line Lamborghini fanatics were outraged to learn that the ugly beast was powered by the same 350hp engine that had been developed for the LP400 Countach. Those who had read their history books knew there were precedents of course: Rolls-Royce had built armored-cars based on the chassis of the Silver Ghost, and the engine developed for the Bugatti Royale was used to power railcars.

The LM001 had fiberglass bodywork built on a tubular chassis. It had a four-wheel-drive transmission system with each wheel independently declutchable, and was equipped with a 5-speed gearbox and limited slip differentials.

The automobile was a bit like a high-powered torpedo-boat that has been converted into a luxury yacht. It had a top speed of nearly 118mph (190kph) and could accelerate from 0 to 62mph (100kph) in only 9 seconds – a remarkable achievement.

The following year, on the occasion of the Monaco Grand Prix, Patrick Mimran unveiled an improved version of his super dune buggy: the LMA (the A stood for *Anteriore,* meaning that the engine was up front). It was driven by a 4.75-liter V12 engine, similar to the one in the Countach LP500S, but its power was held down to 'only' 300hp. It is this improved version, the LMA, that is shown in these pages.

Patrick Mimran knew what he was doing. The LMA prototype was developed and refined over a period of time to become the LM002. This car uses the same engine as the fabulous Countach, reaching 450bhp.

Mimran had also branched out into a profitable sideline manufacturing engines for racing speedboats: superbly efficient V12s with twin overhead camshafts and an engine capacity of between 7 and 8 liters, capable of developing between 550 and 720hp. The rest of the plot is quite easy to imagine.

By 1983, Lamborghini had introduced the LM 004, powered by a 7-liter V12 with a power-rating of 420hp. The 'dune buggy' could now do close to 130mph (210kph) and it could accelerate from 0 to 62mph (100kph) in less than 7 seconds. All you had to do was put your foot down a bit and that Range-Rover behind you disappeared in a cloud of dust.

In spite of their brutally functional appearance, which is probably quite intentional, the Lamborghini LM models are in fact remarkably civilized machines. The suppleness and docility of the V12 Lamborghini engine is guaranteed to charm the most hard-bitten bush driver. As one American motoring writer commented: 'The only

The Countach is an engine mounted on four wheels. The body does very little to hide this fact: the car's lines scream power at the top of their lungs.

effort you have to make when driving the car is to press on the accelerator.'

Yet for the past 15 years, the name of Lamborghini has been firmly identified with the Countach, first shown in 1971.

The Countach is primarily an engine and the marvelous 4.75-liter V12 develops between 375 and 400hp at 7000rpm. Its throaty roar sounds as aggressive as a burst of machine-gun fire, but you can push the rev-counter as far as 8000rpm and the V12 will still sound as smooth and regular as an electric motor. The accelerator pedal that unleashes six double-barreled Weber carburetors is firmer than the clutch pedal on an ordinary automobile but it has all the precision of a micrometer screw-gauge. You can get to the 62mph (100kph) mark in under 5 seconds and if you keep your foot down, the needle reaches the 124mph (200kph) mark only 15 seconds later.

But the Countach is not just an engine. It also has a body, and what a body! This is the first time that a small mid-engined saloon has been given a body that allows the car's personality to assert itself with any conviction. Indeed, the Countach's body does the visual equivalent of announcing its presence with a loud-hailer. With a Porsche or a rear-engined Ferrari, or even the Lamborghini Miura, the car body masses are more or less evenly proportioned fore and aft of the cockpit. The Countach was given a highly unconventional chassis and it ended up with virtually no body mass at all forward of the cockpit. It's all at the rear, where the power-unit causes the body to grow to monstrous proportions and stick out at the back in the manner of a jet-plane's fuselage. The design is unassailably logical.

The Countach's driver sits up front in much the same position as the bombardier in the glassed-in nose of a low-level bomber, and he can see the road racing past just underneath his windshield. The half of the world that stretches out in front of him belongs to him and him alone, but he has to say goodbye forever to everything that is behind him. The minuscule quarter-light windows at the rear are virtually blinded by the air-scoops, and all that is offered by the central rear window (which is in fact more like a gun-slit than a window) is an unforgettable view of the imposing spoiler.

The driver of the Countach finds himself relegated to the front of the car; it is almost like racing along in a jet fighter. He sees the road whistling past just underneath his windshield. You've really got to own a Countach before you discover where the door-handle is: it is hidden up inside the NASA-style air intake.

Mardikian

When you live in Los Angeles and drive a Ferrari, a Lamborghini or a BMW M1, life can be quite frustrating.

The problem is that the speed limit has been set at 65mph (105kph), and the only relief from motoring boredom is the local sport called the 'stoplight Grand Prix': the acceleration race that starts the instant the traffic lights turn green.

Unfortunately, the Ferraris, Lamborghinis and BMWs sometimes get a bit of a surprise.

There is a pretty fair chance that the beaten-up Volkswagen that sidles up beside you at the lights will have a Chevrolet Corvette engine sitting where the back seat should be. An inoffensive-looking Volvo P 1800 S coupé may well be hiding a Ford Mustang V8 engine under its hood. And after a while you learn that it is not wise to tangle with the woman who is off to the shops, proudly driving her Pontiac GTO or her Camaro Z28.

The owner of a Miura or a Boxer who innocently revs up a bit at the lights to clear the cobwebs out of the spark plugs runs the risk of being answered by the devastating roar of a hyperactive V8, egged on by a monstrous GMC 'blower.' Alongside this, your 12-cylinder twin-cam is going to look like that helpless weakling who always gets sand kicked in his face by the Charles Atlas bully on the beach. The only solution left is to turn meekly off the main drag, ears ringing, heart pounding and sweat pouring off you in your little cockpit without air conditioning.

Yes, that's right; the European thoroughbreds, mostly built for sheer speed, are not necessarily going to be open champions of the standing quarter-mile. Especially if they've been weighed down to conform to the US safety standards and are almost choked by the antipollution laws. In Los Angeles they seem condemned to play the role of the tenderfoot who stumbles into a raucous saloon on cowhands' pay-night.

Fortunately, all is not lost. The old hands, over their bourbon, might just condescend to whisper the magic words to the naive youngster sipping his buttermilk: Mardikian, in Newport Beach.

A few sessions of body-building at the Mardikian health-club and the BMW M1 is almost unrecognizable. The elegant coupé has been transformed into a small aggressive saloon with all the muscle it needs to be treated with respect: wide wheels, rear spoiler and twin turbos that will enable it to lay rubber in front of the most arrogant of the 'muscle-cars.

The BMW M1 revised and updated by Mardikian: this is the view that the other drivers get when the traffic lights turn green.

Red velvet and gold-plated telephone: it looks a bit like a gaudy night-club, but in fact it is the rear passenger compartment of the Ferrari 400i limousine, built by Mardikian.

Mardikian is the 'customizer' who has made a specialty of putting a bit more beef under the hood of those wiry little Europeans.

A Ferrari Boxer, a Lamborghini Countach or a BMW M1 will return from a week at the Mardikian health farm boasting twin turbo-chargers, wide rims and a CanAm-style spoiler. And the whole lot will be lavishly decked out in a metallic paint job that would even make one of the more flamboyant young *hombres* from the Mexican quarter jealous.

With a sunroof and air conditioning added, the European machines become more suitable for Californian climes too.

But Mardikian has more tricks up his sleeve. He can build you a Ferrari Daytona convertible . . . that is, if you're not afraid that the ghost of the *Commendatore* will come looking for you one day! After all, the Ferrari in question is a bit blasphemous: it has fiberglass bodywork and a Chevrolet V8 engine with two turbo-chargers. But the combination is an absolute winner: Mardikian's car easily outperforms the original. In fact, the 'customizer' promises a top speed in excess of 199mph (320kph), which is not really surprising given the car's power-rating of 500bhp!

Mardikian can also deliver (at least one year's notice is required) this limousine, based on the Ferrari 400i but with its wheelbase stretched by 75in (190cm). The finished car is an enormous 7.33yd (6.7m) long, which makes it 20in (50cm) longer than a Cadillac Fleetwood!

The limousine's interior is fitted out in a style that is guaranteed to impress even a modern-day Al Capone: the interior is entirely upholstered in red velvet, like a night-club in one of those old 1950s detective movies. Just add a cut-crystal liquor service and a gold-plated telephone, and the illusion is complete.

Just the right car for a modern-day Al Capone in a hurry. Mardikian can turn your Ferrari 400i into a limousine. The wheelbase is stretched by 75in (190cm), making the final car 20in (50cm) longer than a Cadillac Fleetwood. And the 7.33yd (6.7m) monster seems to have as many windows as a railroad wagon. The buyer might just have to lengthen his checkbook to make room for the extra zeros too: the final price is going to come to more than $250,000.

Opel

With its streamlined headrest, the Corsa Spider was making a clear allusion to the style of the open Italian racers of the 1950s.

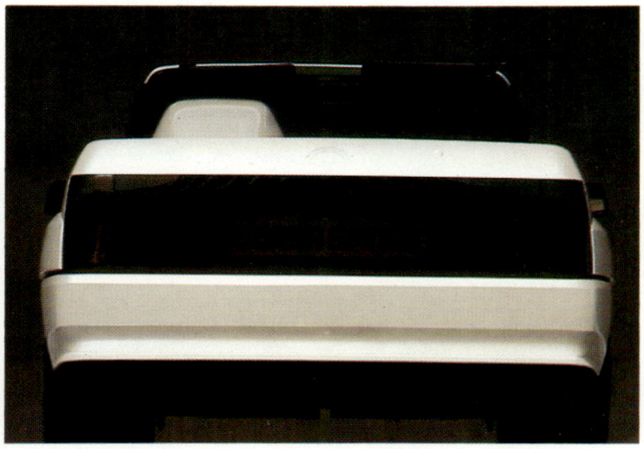

A two-seater roller skate. As a foretaste of the Corsa saloon, Opel presented an amusing and extremely compact little convertible.

The convertible's creator, Georg Gallion, who worked in the Opel design studio, had set out to express the essential characteristics of the sports car, in the most compact form possible. The result was not really a car that you got into, but more a car that you put on, like a pair of tight-fitting slippers.

The roof canopy took up little more space than a foldup plastic raincoat, and slipped out of sight underneath a removable panel. The headlamps and taillights hiding behind smoked-glass screens made the car look as though it was wearing Ray-Bans. And despite the Opel's 3.82yd (3.5m) length, its headrest makes it distinctly reminiscent of the open Italian racers of the 1950s.

For its presentation in front of the public, the Corsa Spider was equipped with the power unit destined for the future Corsa saloon, but it could just as easily accommodate the 2-liter engine from the Kadett GTE.

With the Kadett engine, this little machine, which looked rather like a small white aspirin, was capable of whizzing down the autobahns at close on 124mph (200kph).

Even though it was put on ice once the saloon was ready, the Corsa Spider had allowed the Opel engineers to give full rein to their fantasies – all the better to concentrate on more serious things thereafter . . .

A sports car that looks a bit like a little white pill – but a pill packed full of vitamins. That was what the Opel Corsa Spider was all about. Presented as a preview to the Corsa saloon, it also borrowed the later car's main mechanical elements. But the possibility of a more lively engine (like the Corsa Sprint powerplant) being installed at a later date was certainly not ruled out.

CORSA

Panther

Around 1970, Bob Jankel sold his prosperous textile business to start making the kind of automobiles that he had always wanted to drive.

Rather than continue to supply the shops along Carnaby Street, Jankel decided to make cars for the shops' customers instead. And he was on to a winner: pretty soon every Radio Caroline disc jockey who wanted to stay in business had to drive a Panther as well as wear the obligatory flower-print shirt and flared jeans. And Bob Jankel was there to supply them with an imitation Jaguar SS 100 or a pseudo Bugatti Royale, too.

Emboldened by his success, Jankel decided to build a super-rocket that would guarantee the Panther a permanent place up there in the ranks of prestige automobiles – a car that would keep you one jump ahead even if your neighbor bought a Lamborghini Countach.

Jankel's supercar went on display at the London Motor Show at Earls Court in 1977, and those who came to see it could hardly believe their eyes. Some of them even started counting the wheels on their fingers to make sure they weren't dreaming.

And the sly Bob Jankel, always the business opportunist, had chosen just the right moment: not long before that, the six-wheeled single-seater Tyrrell had been all over the front pages.

The Panther 6 had been given the complete engine and transmission unit out of the front-wheel-drive Cadillac Eldorado. But this time the big V8 was mounted at the rear and twin-turbos had been added. Jankel promised his customers an impressive 600hp to play with. The Panther's interior, with its Ford Capri steering-wheel, smacked of improvisation but it had been equipped with enough gadgets to make even James Bond jealous.

Unfortunately for Bob Jankel, while he was dreaming up his latest Panther, the trendies had started to forsake Carnaby Street and the Liverpool Sound had faded right away to become mere nostalgia. Bob Jankel's ambitious operation went bankrupt.

With its radiator grille in the shape of a rather idiotic grin, Bob Jankel's Panther 6 seems to realize that it looks a bit like a bad joke dressed up as a motorcar.

The dashboard of the Panther 6:
a masterpiece of primitive art.

Pininfarina

He was the Pinocchio of the Farina family, the youngest child who looked as though he had been thrown in for good measure. They had given him the nickname 'Pinin.'

In 1930, the youngest Farina brother founded his own body-styling workshop. And so as to avoid any confusion with his brother's firm, he named it quite simply Pininfarina.

In 1946, Pinin Farina launched the automobile into the jet-age with the rather audacious body that he gave to a Cisitalia chassis: the fenders, the hood, the trunk and the cabin were all brought together into a single harmonious shape, and instead of a radiator grille Farina simply gave it an air intake. The Cisitalia was so logical and worked so well that from that moment onward it became impossible to imagine an automobile looking any other way. And Pininfarina had become the most famous, the most revered and the most sought-after body-shop in the world. Needless to say, the Pininfarina style was also the most-often imitated.

The great Pinin Farina retired in 1958 but he often made midnight inspection visits to the workshops. And when he disapproved of what he saw, he left behind him sarcastic little notes signed with a Napoleonic flourish. By now he was calling himself Pininfarina in one word. In any case, foreign visitors had been spelling it like that for years, completely unaware that at one stage there might have been another Farina to confuse him with.

Giovanni Battista Pininfarina died in 1966. And soon afterward, people began to whisper that Pininfarina designs were starting to look a bit decadent. It is true that the firm had a tendency to rework its previous successes. And while they were doing that, Bertone continued to be as aggressively dynamic as ever. The years rolled by and Pininfarina still had not unveiled anything that could be compared to the Miura, the Marzal or the Carabo.

Then the Modulo was introduced in 1970. The Modulo was designed on the chassis of a Ferrari 512S, but that had very little to do with its suc-

The body of the Modulo is composed of two identical half-shells that are joined one on top of the other in order to make a container for the passengers and the engine. The space between the upper and the lower halves serves to accentuate this composition. The same intention lies behind the 'phony window' that is painted in black as a mirror-image underneath the real window. And was it entirely coincidental that at the very same Turin Motor Show in 1970 Bertone presented the Stratos (see pages 36-38) which went to the same extremes in its radical simplification of automotive forms. In fact, both designers soon felt the need to back away from such extremes. Unlike the Stratos, the Modulo cannot really take to the highways. It should be added here, for it is quite impossible to tell just by looking, that the Modulo is really a Ferrari. But not just any old Ferrari: it is built on the chassis of one of the twenty-five 512S versions that were constructed to meet the challenge of the Porsche 917.

In 1970, Pininfarina unveiled the Modulo, which was the final stage in the evolution that had begun with the 1946 Cisitalia: all of the body elements have been brought together in one single form.

The XJS Spider: in 1978 Pininfarina taught Jaguar a lesson in automotive styling. The lesson is still relevant today.

cess. Pininfarina could have stuck it on to a Fiat 500 chassis just as successfully.

The key is of course the extraordinary lines that Pininfarina gave the Modulo's body: it is quite visibly made up of two symmetrical half-shells stuck together, one on top of the other, to enclose the passengers and the engine.

To underscore this principle, the designers gave the side window a mirror-image directly underneath it: a 'false window' painted in black. The two half-shells do not quite meet at the join; there is a slight gap left between the two that is accentuated by the addition of a red band.

And do you open the Modulo like a packet of cigarettes by pulling on the red cellophane band? Well, almost . . .

The roof panel slides in one piece toward the front, taking the windshield and the side windows with it, rather like an airplane's cockpit canopy. To get into the Modulo, you climb over the rocker panels and stretch out inside as if reclining on a *chaise longue.* The dashboard switches are arranged on a panel that looks like half a rugby ball set beside the gear shifter.

In its own way, the Modulo is the end result of the styling development that began with the Cisitalia in 1946. Every last trace of a separate form for hood, fenders, trunk or cabin has been completely effaced. All that remains is one single shape. To go any farther in radical styling seems almost impossible. And in fact no car has ever gone farther along this road than the Modulo. Even the Pininfarina stylists decided to backtrack from here. And the Modulo is just as futuristic today as it was 20 years ago.

In 1978, Pininfarina had to give Jaguar a lesson in car styling. The people at Coventry had well and truly disappointed their admirers when they presented the horrible XJS coupé as a replacement for the famous XKE. So the Italian bodybuilder showed them how it should have been done by promptly presenting an XJ Spider.

The Pininfarina car evokes the spirit of the XKE Jaguar much more faithfully than the XJS. And the Italians even went as far back as the legendary Le Mans D-Type in their quest for the traditional Jaguar feeling.

Pininfarina had gone right back to the most

With its retractable headlamps and its 'built-in' bumper bars, the XJS Spider could easily pass for an XKE Jaguar stripped down to the bare essentials. You can bet that if one day Jaguar sees fit to bring out an F-Type, then it will be the spitting image of Pininfarina's masterpiece.

quartz
quartz

basic shapes used by the wild cats of Coventry, doing away with the headlamps (they are retractable) and the bumper bars (they are 'invisible' like the ones on the Porsche 928). The car's Sophia Loren curves are also enhanced by widening the Spider's 'hips' just aft of the cockpit.

The English car manufacturer watched this little demonstration with great interest. Would Jaguar decide to start production of the XJ Spider? The idea is still in the air at Coventry even today and Pininfarina's little gem hasn't aged at all.

The story of the Quartz is very like the story of the XJ Spider. By trying to improve on the Audi Quattro, Pininfarina was implicitly singling it out for the firm's 1980 Oscar for ugliness. Indeed, the Audi management was the first to admit that the body of the Quattro was quite unworthy of the engineering marvels that it concealed.

Leonardo Fioravanti, who was Technical Director at Pininfarina, decided to make a homogenous whole out of the Quattro: he would give it a body that was as technically advanced as its powerplant and chassis.

The result was the Quartz, which went on display at the 1981 Geneva Show.

Like the Modulo, the Quartz gives the impression of being composed of two halves, assembled one on top of the other. But this time the designer has completely disregarded the notion of symmetry. The very distinct dividing line between the upper and lower halves of the body is not just there for decoration: it also adds structural strength and houses, in different places, the air intakes and the door handles. And as with the Modulo, this horizontal divider also gives the design a note of refinement. Finally the lower half, which juts out a little all around the body, serves as a wraparound bumper bar.

The Quartz takes full advantage of the aerodynamics research that had been undertaken over the last 10 years by the Pininfarina engineers in the firm's own wind tunnel. In spite of its looks, the Quartz generates a much cleaner airflow than the more spectacular Modulo.

And to cap it all, the Quartz is also an exercise in the use of avant-garde materials: some experimental light alloys, Kevlar, honeycomb, etc. Some of the body panels on the Quartz are of composite construction: a steel-plastic-steel sandwich that is only .04in (1mm) thick. The windows are made of synthetic polycarbonate, which is as hard as glass but more resistant and half the weight. The seats are made out of carbon fiber and resin. The trimmings are 'parachute cloth.' Even the headlamps were designed by Carello.

The end of the tale is reminiscent of the story of the XJ Spider: the Audi management admired the Quartz and had a very close look at it. For a while, the official line was that the German firm would soon begin production of the car, but after a while the idea was quietly shelved.

The Quartz remains Pininfarina's masterpiece of the 1980s. The car is one of those key creations, a reservoir of ideas that creators keep coming back to for inspiration. It is that part of the Quartz's design legacy which can be felt in the Fiat Ritmo Abarth 125TC that Pininfarina presented at the 1983 Geneva Show.

The Quartz: an Audi Quattro that has finally learned how to assert itself as a truly avant-garde automobile.

Rinspeed

The 939: signed by Rinspeed.

White. The car is all white. As white as the milk from the Swiss mountain pastures or the snow up on the alpine peaks.

It should be admitted at the outset that Frank Rinderknecht is Swiss. When choosing a name for the cars he was going to build, he took his own and shortened its wheelbase, lowered it and streamlined it. And where the superfluous syllables had once been he installed a noun that suggested high performance. The word ended up as Rinspeed, a name that is synonymous with luxury, speed and exclusivity.

Rinderknecht did exactly the same thing to his cars.

Whether he is a rock star celebrating his tenth gold record, a collector celebrating the purchase of his twentieth Picasso, or simply the son of an oil emir, the Porsche lover who really wants to buy the best car in the firm's catalogue usually has quite a difficult job choosing between the 911 Turbo, the Carrera convertible and the 928S.

One of the problems is that these three cars have personalities that are far too distinctive for the connoisseur to be content to leave the other two behind, after choosing his favorite. And being able to buy all three of them doesn't make life much simpler either, because even the richest man in the world can only drive one car at a time.

Frank Rinderknecht came up with a solution: it is called the Rinspeed 939.

This stunning machine is to all intents and purposes a synthesis of the three most prestigious Porsche models available. It is a Carrera convertible with the power and transmission unit out of

Three Porsches rolled into one: the Rinspeed 939 is a Carrera convertible with the power unit from the 911 Turbo and some of the bodystyling elements of the 928S.

the 911 Turbo and certain bodystyling elements (bumper bars, quarter panels, headlamps and tail-lights) borrowed from the 928S. But the blending of the three cars is so smoothly executed that the Rinspeed 939 looks as though it was inspired by one single muse.

At the present stage in the evolution of the firm of Porsche, the Rinspeed 939 represents the state of the art: it is the best Porsche possible. The 939 is also, in its own way, a bargain: it costs a little less than the total price-tag of the three factory models that it combines together.

On a lighter note, Frank Rinderknecht must have enjoyed himself immensely turning out this 'Pink Panther' that is really a Suzuki Jimmy, decked in candy pink with silver upholstery. This miniature off-road vehicle (it is only 3.5yd [3.2m] long and 1.53yd [1.40m] wide) is powered by an 800cc engine.

The chromed crash bars and the metallic paint make it seem as though the wind that is ruffling the larch trees has blown all the way from California. A set of special wheels and an assortment of lamps complete the transformation of the car: the Swiss alps have never seen such style before!

Frank Rinderknecht also rewrote the book of rules for the Golf GTi. That was at the 1981 Geneva Show.

The star of the 1981 show was the De Lorean, which was making its first public appearance. With its gull-wing doors raised on high, the De Lorean seemed about to swoop down and devour the spectators. But not far away, over on the Rinspeed stand, there was a sort of miniature De Lorean that seemed to be saying 'Hey, I'm here too . . .'

It was the Rinspeed Aliporta and it, too, had doors that were hinged in the roof panel. The car was based on the Golf GTi but it now had six headlamps, an interior trimmed entirely in Connolly leather, a Porsche 928S dashboard, a stereo fit to blow your ears off and even a refrigerator and a television set for good measure.

The little white marks on the speedometer went right around to 260kph (162mph) and only a few of the marks were there for show. Thanks to the addition of a Rotomaster turbo-charger, the power-rating of the Aliporta's engine had been boosted to 135bhp(DIN), giving a top speed of around 124mph (200kph).

That was the good news; now for the bad. Frank Rinderknecht was asking 100,000 Swiss francs to transform the little Golf, and the customer had to provide his own car to start with!

Today, the Rinspeed Aliporta is still the very last word in Golf GTi's.

A little breeze from over in California has arrived to ruffle the larch trees. This pink candy fantasy, shaped like a car, is in reality a Suzuki Jimmy fully reworked by Rinspeed.

SUZUKI
SUZUKI

The Rinspeed Aliporta. Close the doors and fasten your seat belts. The Porsche 928S speedometer marked up to 260kph (162mph) doesn't exaggerate by much: equipped with a turbo-charged engine, this hyperactive little Golf GTi gives a top speed of around 124mph (200kph).

aliporta

Sbarro

They come from all over the world – from Osaka, Kuwait and Kansas City. They come wearing Stetsons, Arab robes and Pierre Cardin suits. But they're all heading for the same place: Switzerland.

There, in a little village on the edge of Lake Neuchâtel, they confess their innermost fantasies to the only man in the world who can give them concrete expression.

That man makes automobiles. In the village of Tuileries de Grandson, the most far-fetched obsessions are given shape in the form of spoilers and turbo-chargers, fiberglass bodies and metallic paintwork, light-alloy wheels and knotty walnut dashboards.

The man behind all this is Franco Sbarro, a European who beats the Californian 'customizers' at their own game. His clientele is made up of those who no longer have to count their money and for whom money no longer counts, where their abiding passion – motorcars – is concerned. The best there is is not quite good enough for Franco Sbarro's clients: they want the best there could be . . .

Sbarro alone can satisfy their needs, for he shares the very same automotive dreams. To quote Sbarro's own words, as he was not rich enough himself, he chose to use other men's money to build the cars he dreamed about.

Sbarro explains how it works: 'My clients come along to see me. We sit and talk about the subject that we both find passionately consuming: automobiles. When they depart, they take my ideas with them and leave their money behind.'

Franco Sbarro was born in Lecce, a small town in the south of Italy. He moved permanently to Switzerland in 1957 at the age of 18. He started out by repairing tractors and small motorcycles but, like every self-respecting Italian, Sbarro considered that the automobile was the eighth art. His one abiding ambition was one day to build cars that would bear his name.

In 1959, Sbarro bought a small garage and opened a Borgward dealership. When the firm of Borgward disappeared two years later, Sbarro went to work as workshop boss for the BMW dealer in Neuchâtel. It was there that he met Georges Filipinetti, who soon offered Sbarro a job as Director of his motor-racing operations. For the next five years, Sbarro had in his care a flock of Ferraris, AC Cobras, Ford GT40s and Porsche 906s. His work at the head of the *Scuderia Filipinetti* culminated in 1967 with the group's victory in the Le Mans 24-Hour race and also the Targa Florio. Soon afterward, Sbarro decided to regain his independence and finally make his private dream come true.

Sbarro set up shop in a disused cigarette factory near Grandson. The name he chose for his new firm was extraordinarily simple: *Atelier de Construction Automobile* (ACA) or 'car-building workshop.' The badge he chose was rather more eloquent: it showed a greyhound in full flight, like the prewar Lincoln emblem.

Over the last 20 years, more than 300 finished vehicles have rolled out of the Sbarro workshops in Tuileries de Grandson. One single model, the BMW 328 replica that Sbarro introduced in 1974 makes up more than half the firm's total orders. It has been Sbarro's 'bread and butter' car, costing only about as much as a Porsche 944. Yet it would be wrong to talk in terms of a production run: it would be a bit like saying that one of the more prestigious Paris couturiers was in the rag-trade. Sbarro swears that he has never made two 328 cars the same: each vehicle is tailor-made according to the specifications of the individual client in question.

Franco Sbarro greets his visitors dressed in the same faded overalls that his mechanics wear. And he often still has grease on his hands as it is

It was in 1980 that Franco Sbarro built this replica of the Mercedes 540K roadster, a car that was originally produced from 1936 until 1940. The body is made out of fiberglass and the mechanical side is borrowed from a modern Mercedes. The engine is a 5-liter V8 out of the 500 SE that develops 240bhp(DIN) at 4750rpm. Despite the fact that the engine has a V-configuration, the replica has exposed exhaust pipes on only one side of the engine hood, out of respect for the original Mercedes . . . but this time they're for decoration. Sbarro assures his buyers of a top speed of 137mph (220kph). This figure is certainly a little inflated, but there is no doubt that Sbarro's 540K would easily leave for dead the original Mercedes, which was a ton heavier but only had half the horsepower.

he who personally sees to the fine tuning of the engines. And the eyes that peer at you through his spectacles are as sharp as can be: this Italian has garnished his bank account like a true Swiss. He never starts work on a car without a properly drawn-up contract and a sizeable deposit into the bargain.

Over the last 20 years, Sbarro has masterminded an amazing variety of models. Among them are several replicas of the Ford GT40 and a handful of luxury off-road vehicles built for emirs who wanted to go off hunting gazelle with all the modern conveniences to hand. There were also several varieties of outrageously tarted-up Mercedes, complete with turbo-chargers and gull-wing doors hinged in the roof panel. It is also worth mentioning the Stash coupé, Sbarro's curious adventure into the realms of banality. It was almost as if he wanted to prove that he could do absolutely anything, even make a car that was forgettable. And then there was the trick-Golf: the innocent-looking little machine had a Porsche 911 turbo engine hidden at the rear . . .

Between 1936 and 1940, Mercedes took a limited number of 500K and 540K chassis and gave them a singularly attractive roadster body that summed up the whole romantic feeling of motoring in the 1930s: they had long flowing fenders that rose smoothly like waves alongside the enormous hood. The whole thing gave you an incredible sensation of power – much like a battleship that is undergoing its speed trials out in the Baltic Sea.

The car's tiny two-seater cockpit sank its occupants down behind a V-shaped windshield no bigger than the one on a racing airplane. It's the sort of car that you ought to drive in one of those close-fitting leather helmets (white, of course) and goggles, with a long silk scarf streaming out in the wind behind you.

Fifty years later, this is the kind of prestigious supercar that an oil baron (or a soya baron, or a microcomputer baron) will dream of buying when the time comes to announce to the world that he has 'made it.' Then he'll keep a sharp eye out for one of those rare occasions when one of the old Mercedes comes up for auction. When the time comes, it will cost him a cool million dollars of

With its long fenders that surge like waves, its incredibly long hood and its little cockpit stuck down behind a V-shaped windshield, this one car sums up all the glorious romanticism of motoring in the 1930s. That was what the original 540K, built in 1936, was all about, and the same can still be said of the 1980 replica. You have to hand it to Franco Sbarro: he did a superb job. He justly deserved the rare accolade awarded by the old firm of Daimler-Benz: they authorized him to crown his masterpiece with their prestigious three-pointed star.

100
140
kmh
tank

10
20
30
40
50
60
70

The engine of the Royale is really a fake: this is no more than a machined metal casing used to camouflage two 3.5-liter Rover V8 engines.

course, but then that's probably only pocket-money to him anyway.

And then he's in for his biggest surprise. His magnificent new highway cruiser can only just outperform a Pinto: without its turbo-charger, the Mercedes' engine develops no more than 115hp, for an all-up weight of three tons!

If he wants his Valkyrie to sing its battle-song, then he has to bring the turbo-charger into play (by ramming the accelerator hard down), but there are about as many restrictions involved in using the car's turbo as there are attached to pulling the emergency cord on a railroad train.

Alas! his new toy puts up about the same performance against a Golf GTi as a Zeppelin that is being attacked by a fighter plane.

And that's precisely where Franco Sbarro comes into it.

Sbarro displayed his replica of the 540K roadster for the first time at the 1980 Geneva Show. It had a great many admirers and this was one of the rare occasions when the reaction to one of Franco Sbarro's creations was unanimous. Even the renowned firm of Daimler-Benz looked kindly upon the enterprise and authorized Sbarro to affix the prestigious three-pointed star to his car. And that is a favor that the great German firm never accords lightly.

The fiberglass body on the Sbarro 540K is a fairly faithful reproduction of the original. This was a much harder accomplishment than it might seem, as Sbarro had to modify very slightly the car's dimensions in almost every direction in order to accommodate the modern engine and transmission. Both the front and rear track, the wheels themselves, the wheelbase, the length and width of the hood – everything differs that little bit from the original specifications. And Sbarro has carried the whole thing off with magnificent aplomb, for the car has that authentic ring about it.

The Sbarro's engine and transmission have been borrowed from the modern-day Mercedes 500 SE. The car has a 5-liter V8 engine with Bosch fuel injection, an automatic gear box and independent suspension on all four wheels. It accelerates, brakes and holds the road exactly like a modern car and it has a top speed which

Sbarro doing his own remake of the Bugatti Royale is a bit like Cecil B de Mille turning the Bible into a Hollywood epic. It smacks of bad taste being elevated to the status of art. The body styling takes its inspiration from two separate versions of the Royale. The fenders are borrowed from the town coupé that was styled by Binder, and the main body section is based on the Park Ward limousine. There are several 'period' accessories that are worthy of note: the Marchal headlamps, the Bosch klaxons and the friction shock-absorbers.

Royale

The Sbarro Lola T 70 allows a very privileged few to realize what is probably every motorist's secret dream: to drive out on to the highway at the wheel of a real racing car.

betters 124mph (200kph). In spite of the V8 engine under the hood, Sbarro gave the car exposed exhaust pipes on one side only (the American Excalibur did not show the same restraint), but they are still only for decoration.

Sbarro was just as faithful in his reproduction of the original car's aluminum instrument panel with its white-background VDO dials. The Zeiss headlamps are brand new but they are made with the original machine tools.

And when the Sbarro 540K comes up against the Golf or the other GTis it now performs just as well as the original 540K did against the Adlers, the Wanderers and the DKWs of those days.

Franco Sbarro's eyes must have glinted even more mischievously than usual behind his spectacles the day he unveiled 'his' Bugatti Royale at the 1979 Geneva Show.

This was bad taste raised to the status of art. Raise the hood for example – the whole thing lifts up and forward in one piece with supreme disregard for realism. Underneath, you discover not one but two 3.5-liter Rover V8 engines, apparently working in tandem as did the 16-cylinder engines in the Type 45 and 47 Bugattis.

The bodywork of the Sbarro Royale seems to be the result of a blending together of the two original versions of the Royale. The main body section harks back to the limousine body that was styled by Park Ward, and the wings are reminiscent of the town coupé designed by Binder.

The wheels are fairly exact light-alloy reproductions of the originals.

In 1971, Franco Sbarro bought the entire set of machine tooling that had been used to build the Lola T 70 Mark III. His Lola T 70 looks like a manned projectile. Its primary function is to go fast. The ability to reverse into a parking space seems to be a secondary consideration.

The car has no heating and no ventilation. It has no bumper bars and no baggage compartment either: CanAm cars simply didn't need them. By firmly refusing to make any concession to driver comfort, Sbarro has managed to preserve the original character of the car. Of course he did agree to do away with the brutal Chevrolet V8 that powered the original car and offered his clients instead the choice of a Porsche 911 turbo or a 12-cylinder Ferrari engine. Sbarro maintains that his lighter and more streamlined Lolas are faster than the corresponding Porsche and Ferrari; the more finely honed Sbarros can exceed 186mph (300kph).

In 1980, Franco Sbarro turned loose in among the traffic the mechanical equivalent of a piranha: the maximum amount of ferocity confined in the smallest space possible.

The Super Twelve is rather like jamming two motorbikes inside a Mini. Starting with a tubular chassis, Sbarro installed two 6-cylinder Kawasaki motorbike engines (1300cc, 120bhp at 8000rpm), complete with their 5-speed gearboxes and chain transmissions. The engines are coupled together using a drive belt, and each of them drives one wheel, with no differential used at all. The gearboxes are changed simultaneously by a single control rod.

With an enormous 240hp to power a car that weighs only 1764lb (800kg) in full battle kit, the Super Twelve can accelerate from 0 to 62mph (100kph) in under 5 seconds.

The Super Twelve reappeared again in 1984 under the name of Super Eight. This time it only had one engine, but that was the Ferrari 3-liter injected unit (a V8 engine developing 260bhp) out of the 308 GTBi. Needless to say, the car was better off for having swapped engines.

Only Sbarro can go one better than Sbarro . . .

The Lola T 70 is without doubt the most authentic of Sbarro's replicas. And for one very good reason: the bodywork is constructed using the original molds that were bought by Franco Sbarro in 1971. But Sbarro is no traditionalist: he is prepared to equip the car with either a Porsche engine, a Ferrari, a Ford or a Chevrolet, depending on the client's specifications. But whichever engine he finally chooses, the client can rest assured that the car that he is buying will be just as noisy, just as uncomfortable and just as fast as a true racing car.

Super Twelve

The Sbarro Super Twelve is the mechanical equivalent of a piranha: it has as much ferocity as possible packed into the smallest space imaginable. 240bhp is squeezed into a 1764lb (800kg) car that is only 3.39yd (3.10m) long. The mini bomb throws out a challenge at every set of red traffic lights. The exhaust pipes that stick out from the two 6-cylinder Kawasaki engines are ready to blast decibels all over the poor loser.

Vector

A cruise missile built for the highway. It's five o'clock in the morning out on Interstate 15: a ribbon of bitumen, dead straight like a runway, crosses the Mojave desert to the north of Los Angeles.

With the red ball of sun still low down on the horizon, surrounded by the purple mountains, we could be up on Mars. There is not a soul on the road for miles and miles. The Highway Patrol's Cessna is already up there on patrol, humming softly in the quiet air, seeming hardly any bigger than the buzzards that are circling around on the lookout for any stray animal that might have been run over during the night.

Suddenly a black dot appears on the horizon, coming closer and closer with the unreal speed of a video image, disappearing and reappearing from time to time in depressions in the desert flats. The machine is so low slung that instead of driving normally it seems to be sliding along the road surface like an image projected on a screen. No, it's not a stray cruise missile, or a space shuttle making a forced landing. This machine cannot go any faster than Mach 0.3.

For anything that flies, Mach 0.3 is a fairly unimpressive speed. But for a machine that is earthbound it's not bad at all . . . The machine in question is the Vector W2: its mastermind, Gerald Wiegert is out there at the wheel making quite sure that the car will go faster than the 186mph (300kph) or so, promised to his customers. Once his speed trials are over, Wiegert gets on the CB and informs the Highway Patrol that he's finished, and then drives back to Los Angeles at the legal speed limit of 65mph (105kph).

It was in 1976 that the German Gerald Wiegert founded his company Vehicle Design Force. He set up shop in Venice, one of the beachside suburbs of Los Angeles. The real strike force of VDF was to be the Vector Cars Division. Vector's program was quite simple: it set out to build the fastest sports car in the world. This goal might seem a little paradoxical in a country where a low speed limit is such an accepted institution, but the

In spite of appearances, the Vector W2 can hardly go any faster than Mach 0.3; but then that does mean around 186mph (300kph) . . . That wouldn't be very impressive for anything that was designed to fly, but it is a very respectable speed for a machine that is earthbound. The Vector is the brainchild of Gerald Wiegert, who came to California from Germany to build this very Italian-looking small saloon. The Kevlar bodywork hides a V8 Chevrolet engine that can develop 650bhp with the assistance of twin-turbos. An automatic transmission system, designed for dragsters, channels this power down to the road surface with a minimum of power loss. The driver has only to pray that the bitumen is solidly glued to the road!

The Vector has the brutally
functional dashboard of a true
fighting machine.

VECTOR W-2

VECTOR W2

paradox was around long before Wiegert arrived. After all, California has always been one of the major markets for Ferraris, Lamborghinis and Porsches. One of the reasons is that for many customers, high performance also means technical and aesthetic excellence.

Wiegert decided to begin at the beginning. First he took the V8 engine out of a Chevrolet Corvette. Then he gave it twin-turbos and Bosch fuel injection. It was then capable of turning out 650bhp at 6000rpm. Wiegert didn't have to look very far for a transmission system that could handle it. In Los Angeles, which was the hometown of the dragster, any kid who'd got his driver's licence knew that only a B&M 3500 automatic transmission could harness all that power. So the driver of a Vector, simply by pressing down with his right foot, could find out exactly how an astronaut feels at the end of his countdown.

The Vector's body was built of Kevlar around a light-alloy monocoque chassis. The car's lines were unashamedly inspired by Bertone's extraordinary Carabo. But the Italian body-wizard and his brilliant styling chief Marcello Gandini could hardly take offense at this homage that was paid to them, for Wiegert had succeeded in adapting their masterpiece without betraying its soul in any way at all.

As for the interior of the Vector, it could rival the cockpit of a Lockheed SR-71. The matt-black upholstery, the multicolored graphic displays and the no-nonsense rows of switches are conclusive evidence that the Vector is first and foremost a fighting machine.

To start with, the Vector launches an all-out attack on its buyer's bank account. The driver's checkbook is slimmer by at least $150,000 by the time he slips behind the wheel.

In a way, the Vector W2 is Bertone's Carabo adapted to Californian conditions.

Wolfrace

Computer technology and speed – a powerful mix for any modern whizz-kid. The Wolfrace Sonic delivers all this and more. Two of everything – bar a second computer.

It looks like a cross between a dragster and a dune buggy, with a hint of the six-wheel Tyrrell Formula One car. At a glance, it's easy to see that there's more than a touch of the latest and most modernistic technology. Sonic, as the Wolfrace Wheels promotional vehicle is called, was built at the beginning of the 1980s, and some of the features of the car – especially its sophisticated computerized engine/transmission management systems – are only now finding their way into production. Even then they appear only on the most expensive luxury cars.

It was built by ex-aircraft engineer Nick Butler, who built hotrods as a hobby and later turned it into a profession. He began with *Nykilodeon*, a 371 Oldsmobile-engined Bucket T. Even that was ahead of its time, with features and components borrowed directly from Formula One.

It was followed by the even more meticulous Revenge, a classic C-cab which included a number of novel features and established Nick Butler as a major force in customizing and one-off specials. He turned professional, setting up Auto Imagination to design and build anything involved with cars. He had an ambition to build a twin-engined car that remained unfulfilled until Sonic.

Nick Butler is a purist, and takes pleasure in finding solutions to engineering challenges. Sonic was not only a challenge, it also hardly matched most people's perceptions of what a car should be. The money to turn the dream into reality came from Wolfrace Wheels and the genial Barry Treacy. Wolfrace had grown from Treacy's involvement with hotrods and, like Butler, Treacy had built some well-known cars before turning to rodding as his business.

The project was named a Wolfrace product and was designed to have two of everything, including engines. And twice the usual number of problems, too . . .

With six wheels and two V8 engines, the Wolfrace Sonic looks like a cross between a dune buggy and a dragster. Built by Nick Butler, it smacks of the latest in automotive technology.

Placed side by side, each engine is linked directly to the independent rear axle through a separate differential – a technique designed to absorb differences in speed between the two powerplants. But having two independent power sources was still a problem, and Butler solved it by giving Sonic one of its few major solo components – just one computer (if there were two they would never agree about anything).

All of its 100 inputs and 100 outputs are used to full capacity. Just starting the two engines requires 80 pieces of information going in and 90 going out. The engines are started individually, but once they're both fired up the 'sync' control on the push-button dash hands engine balancing over to the computer, and the two V8s work in perfect harmony.

The automatic transmission is push-button operated, but selection of park or reverse requires the simultaneous pressing of two separate buttons, to ensure that it can't be done by accident.

It is street-legal, but hardly ever used; the computer system is easily misled by road situations never envisaged at the design stage, and its 'fail-safe' design means that whenever it's unsure of what's happening it shuts both engines down.

Each of the two cockpits is equipped with a complete dashboard, but there's only one steering wheel.